MASSACHUSETTS

IMPRESSIONS | PHOTOGRAPHY BY PAUL REZENDES

FARCOUNTRY
PRESS

HELENA, MONTANA

Right: Native to North America, the cranberry is a wetland fruit, which means it thrives in bogs such as this one on Nantucket Island.

Facing page: Scenic Guilder Pond in Mount Everett State Reservation in the southern Berkshire Mountains.

Title page: After a hurricane destroyed the original lighthouse on Edgartown Harbor in 1938, a new one was assembled from an existing cast-iron tower and has served the harbor well.

Cover: The community of Sunderland, awash in fall color.

Back cover: Forty miles north of Boston, Rockport is a quaint seaside village on Cape Ann.

ISBN 10: 1-56037-495-0
ISBN 13: 978-1-56037-495-4

© 2009 by Farcountry Press
Photography © 2009 by Paul Rezendes

For more information about our books, write Farcountry Press, P.O. Box 5630, Helena, MT 59604; call (800) 821-3874; or visit www.farcountrypress.com.

Created, produced, and designed in the United States.
Printed in China.

13 12 11 10 09   1 2 3 4 5 6

Right: The House of the Seven Gables was built in 1668 and is one of New England's oldest surviving wooden mansions. Other historic structures have been relocated to the site, including the birthplace of Nathaniel Hawthorne, who immortalized the grand home in his novel by the same name.
PHOTO BY SUSAN COLE KELLY

Below, left and right: It seems only appropriate for Springfield—the city where Theodor Seuss Geisel was born and raised—to develop the Dr. Seuss National Memorial Sculpture Garden. The park is filled with whimsical bronze sculptures depicting characters in the author's beloved books.
PHOTOS COURTESY OF THE SPRINGFIELD MUSEUMS, SPRINGFIELD, MASSACHUSETTS

Left: This bronze statue of Massasoit, Great Sachem ("Leader") of the Wampanoags, stands in Plymouth. In 1621, he entered into a peace treaty with John Carver, the first governor of the Plymouth Colony, which lasted for many years.

Far left: The sparkle of holiday lights invites locals to stroll through Boston's Faneuil Hall Marketplace. PHOTO BY SUSAN COLE KELLY

Below: A bronze bas-relief at the base of the Pilgrim Monument in Provincetown shows the new colonists lining up to sign the Mayflower Compact in 1620, establishing a basis for a government for their new settlement. Forty-one Pilgrims signed the document—all were male, as women were not allowed to sign.

These pages: Reenactments of the April 19, 1775, Battles of Lexington and Concord that started the Revolutionary War are held in Concord's Minute Man National Historical Park. The night after Paul Revere's ride and following a morning skirmish on the Lexington village green, 500 patriots on the North Bridge routed three companies of British soldiers. PHOTOS BY SUSAN COLE KELLY

Facing page: Spring foliage provides the backdrop for the scenic Millers River near Wendell.

Below, left: Whitmore Falls near Sunderland attracts visitors to its refreshing waters and lush vegetation.

Below, right: Townsend's Willard Brook State Forest contains 2,597 acres of New England hardwoods and tumbling brooks.

Quiet seems to wash over the northern Berkshire Mountains, seen here from the Mohawk Trail at dusk.

Right: Granville State Forest in southern Massachusetts invites visitors to explore its 2,426 acres. Once the hunting and fishing grounds of the Tunxis tribe, the rolling terrain later became open pastures and farmland before slowly transforming to the dense forest that it is today.

Below: Beavers have chosen an exquisite spot to build their dam, along a tributary of the Squannacook River near Townsend. The river is part of the Nashua River watershed.

Left: Dairy cows graze in a pasture at the base of the Mount Holyoke Range, volcanic mountains that spread east and west across the Connecticut River Valley. Hikers enjoy the many miles of trails that crisscross its terrain.

Below: Growing abundantly in marshes, blue-joint grass along Lawrence Brook near Royalston provides a lush, green carpet of vegetation.

Left: Rowes Wharf, on the Boston waterfront, has a long history: In the 1700s, John Rowe filled his shops and warehouses with exotic imported goods. Over the next century, packet ships and steamships dominated the harbor's waters. The 1900s saw a gradual revitalization of the declining waterfront, which now caters to tourism and upscale commercial ventures. PHOTO BY SUSAN COLE KELLY

Below, left: When Chubby and Bessie Woodman opened a roadside shack on the Essex causeway in 1914, they couldn't have foreseen the enduring popularity of the fried clam, which their eatery introduced during a Fourth of July celebration in 1916. PHOTO BY SUSAN COLE KELLY

Below, right: Still family owned, Woodman's of Essex also offers lobsters, other seafood delicacies, and "clambakes to go" from its Main Street location. PHOTO BY SUSAN COLE KELLY

Above: The diminutive saw-whet owl, only about seven inches tall, is the smallest of the eastern owls. It is a treat to catch a glimpse of this nocturnal hunter.

Top right: This bobcat kitten has ventured from its den into the sun-dappled forest. About twice the size of a domestic house cat, the female bobcat has one litter, usually of two kittens, each year.

Bottom right: Woodchucks (also known as groundhogs) are active during the day and are common in both urban and rural settings. Members of the marmot family, they're true hibernators, sleeping in burrows from October to early spring—although they're occasionally roused on February 2 to find out just when spring will begin.

Facing page: Titled *Freedom from Want,* this familiar painting hangs in the Norman Rockwell Museum in Stockbridge and is part of the artist's famous four-part "Freedom" series, inspired by a speech by Franklin D. Roosevelt.

Left: Intriguing ice formations fill Falmouth Harbor on Cape Cod after unusually cold temperatures.

Below: A cold spell creates an icy wonderland at Cape Cod Bay.

Right: The Atlantic White Cedar Swamp Trail, part of the Cape Cod National Seashore trail system, offers a shaded boardwalk winding through one of the Cape's few remaining stands of Atlantic white cedar.

Below: High Ledges, a wildlife sanctuary near Shelburne, protects a wide variety of wild native plants, such as this delicate yellow lady's slipper, member of the orchid family.

These pages: **A visit to Old Sturbridge Village is a trip back in time. Visitors to the Northeast's largest outdoor history museum explore dozens of carefully restored buildings and watch costumed re-enactors carry out the activities of daily life in an early nineteenth-century community.**
PHOTOS COURTESY OF OLD STURBRIDGE VILLAGE, STURBRIDGE, MASSACHUSETTS

Above: Thatched-roof houses, raised-bed gardens, and other elements of early colonial life have been recreated in Plimoth Plantation (the most common spelling used by Governor William Bradford in his history of the colony). Other features of the plantation include a Wampanoag homesite and, a few miles to the north, a reproduction of the *Mayflower.* PHOTO BY SUSAN COLE KELLY

Right: The *Lagoda,* a half-scale ship, is one of the many attractions at the New Bedford Whaling Museum, which is devoted to bringing to life the era when sailing ships dominated merchant trade and whaling. PHOTO BY SUSAN COLE KELLY

Left: Covering 39 square miles and offering 181 miles of shoreline, the Quabbin Reservoir, pictured here at New Salem, is one of the largest manmade bodies of water in the country. From June until September, golden hedge-hyssop brightens its shores.

Below: Also producing yellow blooms in the summer months, the horned bladderwort grows in wet environments such as this bog in Petersham's Harvard Pond. The carnivorous plant has a bladder that traps tiny aquatic animals that supplement its nutrient requirements.

Right, top and bottom: **The age-old New England tradition of tapping sugar maple trees for their sap usually begins in early February. Farmers head into the woods with buckets to gather the sap, which they boil and convert into pure maple syrup.**
PHOTOS BY SUSAN COLE KELLY

Far right: **An early spring snow coats the shoreline of the East Branch of the Swift River in Petersham.**

Above: The tranquil and charming Hadley Harbor sees boats under sail come and go, some on their way to explore the nearby Elizabeth Islands.

Left: Boats find an inviting place to moor at Nantucket Harbor. In the summertime, the population of Nantucket, located thirty miles south of Cape Cod, more than quadruples with tourists and summer residents.

Facing page: Many folks who take a ride on one of the Swan Boats in Boston's Public Garden don't realize that the iconic boats were created in 1877 by Robert Paget, who designed a paddleboat with a swan at the stern to provide some cover for its captain. Each boat holds about twenty passengers, and Paget's family still owns the popular operation. PHOTO BY SUSAN COLE KELLY

Below, left: This statue of Paul Revere on horseback was erected within sight of the Old North Church, which was built in 1723. On the night of April 18, 1775, two lanterns were hung from its bell tower as a signal to Paul Revere (and poor forgotten William Dawes) to begin his legendary ride warning locals that the British Army was arriving by sea—or more accurately, the Charles River. PHOTO BY SUSAN COLE KELLY

Below, right: The brick row-houses on cobblestoned Acorn Street in Boston's Beacon Hill were built in the late 1820s. Fashionable Beacon Hill has been home to many famous residents, including John Hancock, Louisa May Alcott, Robert Frost, and Senator Edward M. Kennedy. PHOTO BY SUSAN COLE KELLY

Right: The Connecticut River flows through western Massachusetts, making the surrounding valley some of the most productive farmland in New England.

Below, left: In the 1870s, Bostonians supported the construction of a new Trinity Church in Copley Square. For the marshy soil to support the immense weight of the Romanesque structure's granite and sandstone, an elaborate foundation of wooden piles had to be built. PHOTO BY SUSAN COLE KELLY

Below, right: After studying in Italy, sculptor Thomas Ball returned to the United States and spent four years—1860 to 1864—laboring over the equestrian statue of George Washington that overlooks the Boston Public Garden. PHOTO BY SUSAN COLE KELLY

Left, top: The original nineteenth-century lighthouse at Clark's Point led sailors safely into New Bedford Harbor during the height of the whaling trade. In the 1860s a seven-sided granite fort was built on the site to protect Union shipping during the Civil War.

Left, bottom: The *Mayflower II*, with its hand-colored maps, historical navigation tools, and tarred hemp rigging, was designed to give visitors a sense of what it would have been like to sail aboard a seventeenth-century vessel. The smaller boat moored at its side, called a shallop, would have been used for coastal exploration and other maritime work.

Facing page: Established in 1968, the Nantucket Shipwreck and Lifesaving Museum preserves the memory of the many brave islanders who have risked their lives to save others as countless vessels floundered in Nantucket's often dangerous waters.

Right: Black birch trees drop their golden leaves along a walkway at Walden Pond, made famous by writer and resident Henry David Thoreau. Today, Walden Pond, which is designated a National Historic Landmark, is considered by many to be the genesis of the conservation movement.

Far right: Brilliant fall color adorns the streets of Petersham, incorporated in 1754. Thousands of acres of public land flank the town.

PHOTO BY SUSAN COLE KELLY

Right: The attractive stone grist mill operated by the Wayside Inn in Sudbury was commissioned by automaker Henry Ford and was first put to use in 1924. The mill produced ground corn, wheat, and rye for many years and continues to market its products today.

Below, left: Although a statue of Roger Conant stands outside the Salem Witch Museum in Salem, this early resident actually founded the town with a group of fishermen more than sixty-five years before the Salem Witch Trails of 1692. PHOTO BY SUSAN COLE KELLY

Below, right: The Gloucester Fisherman's Memorial features an eight-foot-tall rendering of a fisherman dressed in oilskins and braced at the wheel of his ship. The statue overlooks Gloucester Harbor, where many fishermen have lost their lives to the sea. PHOTO BY SUSAN COLE KELLY

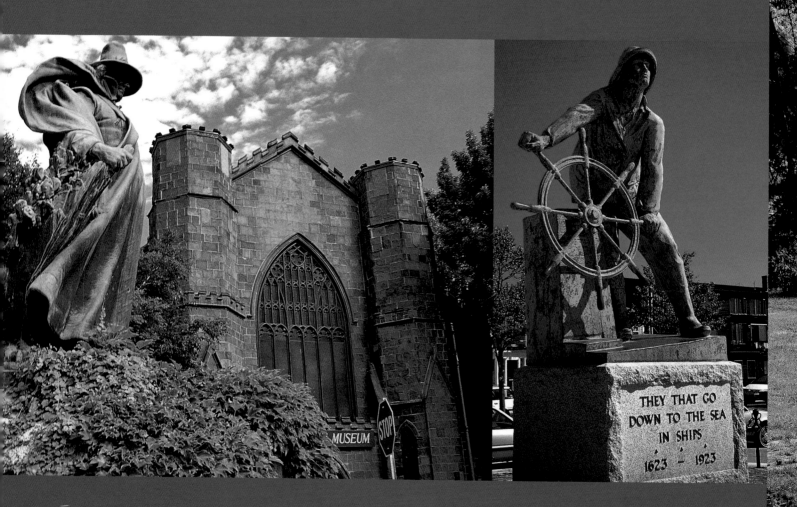

THEY THAT GO
DOWN TO THE SEA
IN SHIPS
1623 – 1923

Facing page: A patchwork of parcels, including hardwood and conifer forests, marshes, open fields, and brush land, make up the Birch Hill Wildlife Management Area in north-central Massachusetts. These 7,400 acres aid conservation efforts for the Millers River watershed.

Below, left: Spring returns to the Rutland Brook Wildlife Sanctuary, a 1,500-acre protected area in central Massachusetts known as an excellent place to spot porcupines, otters, and, later in the year, an orchid known as the nodding ladies' tresses.

Below, right: A small stream winds through boulders on the Mount Tom State Reservation, near Holyoke. Popular with hikers, the traprock mountain is known for its dramatic views above the surrounding Connecticut River Valley.

Right: The sun sets on the Annisquam Light, completed in 1801 to illuminate the entry to the Annisquam River at Wigwam Point. In 1897 the original wooden tower was replaced with a brick structure. The lighthouse may be reached from the nearby village of Annisquam in Gloucester.

Below: A spectacular sunrise brings vivid color to the still waters of Martha's Vineyard. Accessible only by sea or by air, Martha's Vineyard is New England's largest resort island.

Right: Opening day at Fenway Park on April 20, 1912, began a legend etched in the hearts of many Boston Red Sox fans. The 7–6 defeat of the New York Highlanders (the future Yankees) handed out by the Red Sox might have gained more notice had the *Titanic* not hit an iceberg five days before. PHOTO BY SUSAN COLE KELLY

Facing page: Every serious runner dreams of participating in the Boston Marathon, the world's oldest continually run marathon. The first race was organized in 1897, and in 1927 the course was lengthened to the full 26.22 miles. The race is held on Patriots' Day, which commemorates the Battles of Lexington and Concord that began the Revolutionary War. Originally April 19, the holiday's date is now the third Monday of April. PHOTO BY SUSAN COLE KELLY

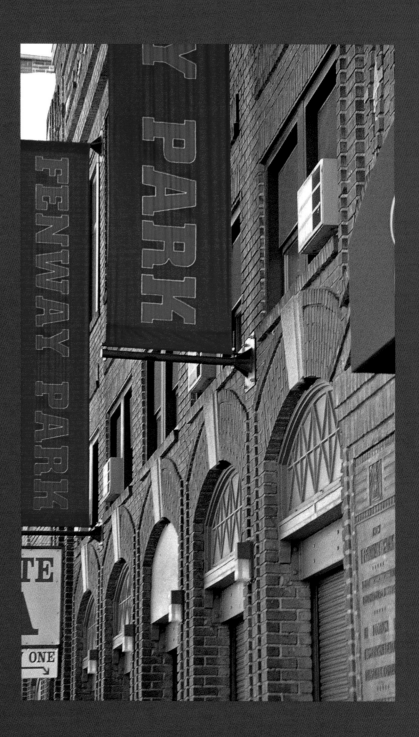

51

Facing page: Basalt cliffs in the Mount Tom State Reservation near Holyoke offer grand views of the valley below. The basalt ridges, often fractured by erosion into dramatic formations, are the result of several massive lava flows that occurred over millions of years.

Below: The Red Apple Farm in Phillipston got its start in the mid-1700s. Still a working farm, it is home to the oldest commercially planted Macintosh apple tree in New England, planted in 1912.

Many visitors to Martha's Vineyard are surprised to learn of the strong presence of Native Americans on the island. The ancestors of the Wampanoag people have populated the island for at least 10,000 years, fishing and growing crops. The Aquinnah Cliffs, also known as the Gay Head Cliffs, are composed of colorful layers of sediment deposited by ancient glaciers. They have a sacred place in Wampanoag history.

Right, top: **Fertile land along the Connecticut River in Whately encouraged colonists' agricultural enterprises. Other natural resources such as clay, lumber, and water allowed the development of brick makers, builders, and small mills.**

Right, bottom: **Spring visits Hardwick, located in the highlands northwest of the Ware River corridor. When industrial ventures declined in the early twentieth century, Hardwick returned to an agricultural economy based on poultry, dairy, and farming.**

Far right: **The West Branch of the Tully River glides by a scenic red barn and fall foliage in the village of Tully.**

Above, left: The Bunker Hill Monument, begun in 1827 but not dedicated until 1843, memorializes the first major Revolutionary War battle. The monument is built entirely from granite quarried in Quincy, and the battlefield, except the hill's summit, had to be sold to pay for it. PHOTO BY SUSAN COLE KELLY

Above, right: Although most of the academic and office buildings at the Massachusetts Institute of Technology are locally known by numbers, the first buildings constructed on the Cambridge campus are officially called the MacLaurin Buildings. Completed in 1916, they include the graceful Great Dome. PHOTO BY SUSAN COLE KELLY

Left: Crossing the Taunton River was made easier with the construction of the Braga Bridge. Its high middle span allows ocean-going vessels access to the busy shipping channel. Directly below the bridge lie Battleship Cove and the USS *Massachusetts*, renowned battleship of World War II.

Right: Another picturesque lighthouse is found at Nobska Point at Woods Hole. The deep harbor in this location saw a significant whaling fleet in the early nineteenth century, with a lighthouse established in the 1820s. Some fifty years later the lighthouse was rebuilt as a forty-foot cast-iron tower.

Below: Anglers get an early start on a day of fishing at Nauset Marsh near Eastham. In addition to its many species of fish and other marine life, the marsh serves as an important habitat for waterfowl and shore birds.

Right: Sandy dunes, a bike trail, and fishermen's access are important features of Province Lands, located at the north end of Cape Cod National Seashore. A visitor center and a lighthouse also invite folks to learn about the area and admire the ever-changing vistas.

Below: Families find Wingaersheek Beach at North Gloucester hard to resist. Here, hermit crabs hide in tidal pools, rocks beg to be climbed on the edge of the beach, and sand dollars wait to be found. PHOTO BY SUSAN COLE KELLY

Left: Snowy woodlands are reflected in the still waters of New Salem's Bow Brook in the Quabbin Reservation. The reservation houses the Quabbin Reservoir, a massive public-drinking-water reservoir, as well as 56,000 acres of mostly forested watershed land and an extensive network of trails.

Below: Glacial potholes at the base of Salmon Falls fascinate observers. When the last glaciers melted eons ago, the swollen Deerfield River began to carve these intriguing shapes into the metamorphic rock.

Above: Campers at wooded Lake Dennison may enjoy a predawn hike or take their mountain bikes into adjacent Birch Hill Wildlife Management Area, which offers diverse habitats for flora and fauna.

Left: The sun illuminates a gentle mist over the Little River at Newbury. A tributary of the Parker River, the Little River flows through both urban areas and quiet salt marshes. For many years the moving

Right: Quartzite crags, a type of metamorphic rock, allow climbers to explore Monument Mountain in the Berkshires. The mountain has a long literary history, including a fortuitous first meeting between authors Nathaniel Hawthorne and Herman Melville in the summer of 1850.

Below: Cambridge's Harvard University, the oldest institution of higher learning in the United States, was founded just sixteen years after the arrival of the Pilgrims at Plymouth. Although many of its early graduates became Puritan ministers, seven U.S. presidents also received degrees from the university. PHOTO BY SUSAN COLE KELLY

These pages: Early Methodists first came to Martha's Vineyard to attend summer revivals and listen to sermons. As the revivalists expanded their summer retreats, they began building a medley of colorful cottages with a unique architectural style and gingerbread scrollwork in a village that became known as Oak Bluffs. Today Oak Bluffs enjoys a lively tourist trade.

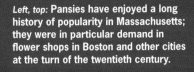

Left, top: **Pansies have enjoyed a long history of popularity in Massachusetts; they were in particular demand in flower shops in Boston and other cities at the turn of the twentieth century.**

Left, bottom: **The Massachusetts state flower, the mayflower, trails across the ground and produces delicate pink or white blooms in the spring.**

Far left: **Painstakingly restored over a two-year period, the Jonathan Young Windmill on Cape Cod retains its original mechanical parts. Built in the early 1700s in South Orleans, the windmill was moved to Town Cove in 1839.**

Right: Located in north-central Massachusetts on the New Hampshire border, Ashburnham was officially incorporated in 1765. Although the town has experienced recent growth, it still retains a rural character.

Below, left: Roses climb the weathered siding of an old barn in Athol, near the Millers River.

Below, right: Among the holiday decorations in Historic Deerfield is a wreath on the door of the Wilson Printing House, a nineteenth-century business that moved a number of times before returning to its original location.

Left: Stormy skies highlight the Cape Poge Wildlife Refuge and connecting Cape Poge Elbow on Chappaquiddick Island. Birders and anglers find many species to satisfy their venture to the shore.

Below: The day comes to a close on Martha's Vineyard in the Vineyard Haven Harbor.

spired by his lifelong love of nature, Paul Rezendes
ecializes in large-format North American landscapes
d seascapes, with a special emphasis on his native
ew England. He is the author/photographer of several
oks, including the best-selling *Tracking and the Art*
Seeing; The Wild Within: Adventures in Nature and
nimal Teachings; Wetlands: The Web of Life, coauthored
th his wife, Paulette Roy; *Martha's Vineyard Seasons;*
d *The Lighthouse Companion* series. His photographs
ve been featured in hundreds of books, magazines,
d calendars. When not traveling by all-wheel-drive van
thirty-foot sailboat, Paul lives with his wife in a remote
rest on the Millers River in Athol, Massachusetts.

ckground: The surf continues its timeless ebb and flow at the
pe Cod National Seashore.